THE ANATOMY OF HYMNODY

THE ANATOMY OF HYMNODY

Austin C. Lovelace

ABINGDON PRESS

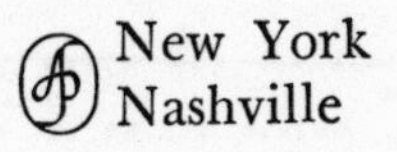

New York
Nashville

THE ANATOMY OF HYMNODY

Library of Congress Catalog Card Number: 65-10550

SET UP, PRINTED, AND BOUND BY THE PARTHENON PRESS, AT NASHVILLE, TENNESSEE, UNITED STATES OF AMERICA

PREFACE

A hymn can be defined as a poetic statement of a personal religious encounter or insight, universal in its truth, and suitable for corporate expression when sung in stanzas to a hymn tune. Perhaps few forms of poetry are so widely known and used, and so generally misunderstood and unappreciated. The hymn is one of the most difficult of all poetic forms to master, for its small palette and vast subject matter make demands on technique which give pause to the great poets yet seem to encourage the versifiers—those carefree souls who "have a feel for meter" and "can rhyme," even though the results are doggerel.

A look at the horizon of hymnody reveals a small number of masters of the art of hymn writing, with Isaac Watts and Charles Wesley towering over all the landscape. Without a doubt, one of the chief reasons for the popularity of Watts and Wesley lies in their ability to express lyrically as well as simply the Christian's experience. Both men had a classical education, which meant they knew Greek and Latin (and Hebrew), understood the root meanings of words, and were thoroughly schooled in the meters and niceties of poetic expression. In the introduction to *Songs of Praise Discussed* Percy Dearmer explains the subsequent decline in hymn quality: "The principle of poetry was lost sight of, it was forgotten that the object of a hymn is to *express* and not define—to be, in fact, like the Gospels."

The modern horizon of hymnody reveals only an occasional molehill, for the past fifty years has not been notable for its contributions to the field of hymnody. It has been said that the chief contribution of the church in latter days has been the mimeograph machine. Perhaps it is true that our concern has been mass media, lifting up emphases and projects, and in general being activists rather than artists.

Yet there are encouraging signs in church architecture which reveal a careful restudy of the relationship of art to theology, of form to meaning, which may indicate that a new day is at hand in the church's understanding and use of art forms. If a revival of hymnody is to occur, there must be a new study and understanding of the relation of the forms of poetry to the subject matter of hymnody. And it is toward a better understanding on the part of clergy, musicians, and congregations that this small book is directed.

If the title sounds a bit strange, the choice is intentional. A hymn is not an amorphous bit of spiritual protoplasm designed for the enjoyment of the man in the pew and for the creation of a pious feeling or a "religious mood." Like the human body, a hymn has a skeleton (which can be called the metrical design) and characteristics determined by the choice of poetic "foot." It is a complete body, made up of several parts (stanzas), each with its definite function. Its visage or physiognomy is determined by the poetic devices the poet chooses. Underlying all the physical features, however, is the soul of the hymn—man's response to God. It is the author's hope that this book may make the reader aware of the structure of hymnody as a guide toward directing his thoughts to the spirit and soul of hymnody.

AUSTIN C. LOVELACE

CONTENTS

I. PROSODY AND RHYME

In any course on hymnology there is always a fleeting reference to such words as "iambic," "trochaic," and maybe even "dactylic" and "anapaestic." The enigma of CM, SM, LM, D, and assorted numbers is partially cleared up, and perhaps the number of syllables in each line of poetry counted. This is about the extent of the explanation. The important question is, "Why does a poet choose one pattern of accent rather than another for his hymn?" Is there, for example, a real difference in mood and emotional impact between iambic and trochaic which makes one preferable for a given type of text? Is there some valid reason, whether consciously recognized by the poet, why Long Meter is chosen instead of Short Meter for a particular subject? Is it possible that the vague feeling of unhappiness or inappropriateness sometimes felt toward a hymn is related to the use of wrong accents and meter?

A recent experience brought focus to the problem. A music editor requested an anthem arrangement of a fuguing tune by Daniel Read (American, 1757-1836) and suggested that a text for Lent would be appropriate because of the minor tonality and the character of the music. A search through several hymnals revealed only one Lenten hymn in Common Meter, the metrical design of Read's tune. That text was "There is a green hill far away," obviously not a meditative or subjective text which would fit the fuguing tune. This discovery raised the question: Why do poets not use Common Meter for Lenten devotional hymns? An attempt will be made to find a satisfactory answer.

All poetry is organized into "feet," indicating that poetry "walks" or "marches." A "foot" consists of a group of two or more syllables with one accented and the others unaccented. In classical poetry the number of feet was important; e.g., iambic pentameter meant five groups of feet with the pattern of ∪ /. Today we count the number of syllables in a line, rather than the feet, and we call the group of numbers which make a stanza the meter. Hence

Common Meter (CM) is a convenient way of saying there are eight syllables (actually four iambic feet) in lines one and three, and six syllables (three iambic feet) in lines two and four, or 86.86. Long Meter (LM) is 88.88; Short Meter (SM), 66.86. D indicates "Double," or repetition of the pattern. Hence CMD is 86.86.86.86. Beyond these most frequently used meters numbers are used to indicate the number of syllables in each line of poetry, e.g., 87.87.

The most common form in English poetry is the iambic foot, consisting of an upbeat (◡) followed by an accent (/)—◡ /.. It is the basis of Long Meter, Common Meter, Short Meter (and their doubles), plus such assorted patterns as 66.66.88., 86.886., 88.88.88., and 10 10.10 10. Iambic movement is stately and noble and is best used for those texts which are propositional. The upbeat pattern before each accent allows time for an idea to start development and to reach its climax in a towering peak at the end of a series of rolling hills. It can also be likened to the roll of the ocean, a series of cresting waves ending in a gigantic wave pounding the shore. Its basic usage is exposition:

◡ / ◡ / ◡ / ◡ /
O God, our help in ages past.

The trochaic pattern is the reverse of iambic, starting with an accent and relaxing on the second pulse (/ ◡). It is more direct than iambic and is used where directness of thought and excitement are desirable. It is not by chance that Charles Wesley used trochaic for "Hárk! thĕ hérăld angels sing" and "Christ the Lord is risen today" for the two great festivals of the Christian year.

The pure classic dactylic (/∪∪) is a comparative rarity in modern hymnody, and is difficult to set musically because of the two final unaccented syllables. Perhaps the best known example is, "Worship the Lord in the beauty of holiness." Closely related is anapaestic (∪∪/), although it is usually altered by shortening a foot somewhere in the line. "Immortal, invisible, God only wise" technically can be considered anapaestic since it ends with the accented syllable; yet its feeling is more dactylic after the first syllable, "Im-." Both meters are used for exuberant, ecstatic texts, for a feeling of lightness comes from the use of the basic triplet movement. More will be said of Wesley's use of these patterns in a later section.

The following illustration will perhaps make clear the wide gulf of feeling which separates anapaestic from iambic. Can one imagine

> 'Twas the night before Christmas and all through the house
> Not a creature was stirring, not even a mouse.

put in iambic Common Meter?

> 'Twas Christmas eve, the house was still,
> And not a creature stirred.

One other meter is occasionally found in most hymnals—the sapphic. It is listed as 11 11 11.5., but each of the elevens is subdivided into a combination of five and six syllables, the five being a combination of a dactyl and a trochee, and the six being entirely trochaic. It was a favorite of Latin hymn writers.

> Father, we praise Thee, now the night is over;
> Active and watchful, stand we all before thee;
> Singing, we offer prayer and meditation;
> Thus we adore thee.[1]

Another example from the German tradition is Johann Crüger's

> Ah, holy Jesus, how hast thou offended,
> That man to judge thee hath in hate pretended?
> By foes derided, by thine own rejected,
> O most afflicted! [2]

The forcefulness of the accented beginnings and trochaic endings is tempered by the break in pattern, thus providing intense meditative qualities.

Two other meters, the elegiac and alcaic, are seldom found. The elegiac was used by Venantius Fortunatus for his sixth-century processional hymns, usually translated "Hail thee, Festival Day; Blest day, that are hallowed for ever." (See *The Hymnal 1940 Companion,* No. 86, and particularly *Songs of Praise Discussed,* p. 212, for a discus-

[1] From *The English Hymnal,* by permission of Oxford University Press. Unless otherwise noted hymns cited as examples are from either *The Pilgrim Hymnal* or the 1935 edition of *The Methodist Hymnal.*

[2] From *The Yattendon Hymnal,* by permission of Oxford University Press.

sion of the variants of the elegiac meter.) About the only example available of alcaic is found in *Songs of Praise,* No. 236, "O saint of summer, what can we sing for you." The cretic (/ ᴗ /) is short, staccato, and strong: "On this day earth shall ring." The spondee (//) with only two syllables is extremely rare. For all practical purposes the most popular congregational hymnody has been limited to iambic, trochaic, and variations on dactylic and anapaestic.

If the rhythmic life and vitality of a hymn is created by the meter, the memorability is aided by rhyme. Clement Wood gives this definition: "Rhyme is the identity in sound of an accented vowel in a word, usually the last one accented, and of all the consonantal and vowel sounds following it; with a difference in the sound of the consonant immediately preceding the accented word." [3] While some rhyming words may be spelled alike (love-dove), they may also be spelled differently (ate, bait, straight, freight). Conversely, identically spelled words may be pronounced differently (cough, enough, plough, though, through).

Rhyming is not a particularly difficult operation—it takes little imagination to rhyme "June" with "moon"; but the good hymn writer succeeds in making the rhymes sound and feel natural, not forced or obvious. The poor writer finds his thought patterns being forced into uninspired channels by facile and overly familiar rhymes.

[3] Clement Wood, *The Complete Rhyming Dictionary* (Garden City: Garden City Books, 1936), p. 25.

Rhyme at its best stimulates the imagination; at its worst it degenerates into doggerel.

Some combinations of words are known as "eye rhymes" because they look alike but are pronounced differently. "Earth" and "hearth" look fine on paper but are false rhymes.

"Identities" are combinations of words which have the same consonant before the final accented vowel. In true rhyme the consonant which precedes the accented vowel must be different according to the definition of rhyme:

say-assay
bay-obey
laying-delaying

Occasionally the finest poet will work himself into a corner which can only be avoided by the use of a "false rhyme" or an "almost rhyme"; but before condemning them one should remember that some apparently false rhymes may have been correct in earlier usages and pronunciations. Charles Wesley consistently rhymed "joined" with "mind," for both were pronounced alike in his day.

The following false rhymes are probably never noticed by a congregation singing "Come, Thou long-expected Jesus," by Charles Wesley:

Jesus-release us
deliver-forever
Spirit-merit

Consonance, sometimes called "off rhymes," is created by having all of the consonants and vowel sounds after the accented vowel identical, but with the accented vowels different:

Spirit-merit (ih and eh)
heaven-given (eh and ih)
cunning-winning (uh and ih)

Assonance, also called "vowel rhyme," has an identical final accented vowel sound, but with dissimilar subsequent sounds:

bliss-is (s and z)
praise-grace (z and s)

Jan Struther has written a hymn which relies entirely on similarity of sounds and has no true rhymes:

We thank you, Lord of Heaven,
For all the joys that greet us,
For all that you have given
To help us and delight us
In earth and sky and seas;
The sunlight on the meadows,
The rainbow's fleeting wonder,
The clouds with cooling shadows,
The stars that shine in splendour—
We thank you, Lord, for these.[4]

While an occasional false rhyme can be used without serious damage, the widespread acceptance of assonance

[4] From *Songs of Praise, Enlarged Edition*, © 1931, renewed 1959, by permission of Oxford University Press.

and consonance as a replacement for rhyme is highly unlikely in hymnody, since they are insufficient aids to the memory.

The usual rhyming patterns are found at the ends of lines of poetry. (A single line is technically a *verse;* a series of lines makes a *stanza.*) In a four-line stanza the best poets will have two pairs of rhymes—rhyming couplets:

> Jesus, where'er Thy people meet, A
> There they behold Thy mercy seat; A
> Where'er they seek Thee Thou art found, B
> And every place is hallowed ground. B

or cross rhyme:

> Come, Holy Spirit, heavenly Dove, A
> With all Thy quick'ning powers; B
> Kindle a flame of sacred love A
> In these cold hearts of ours. B

Alfred Tennyson was fond of an ABBA rhyme scheme as shown in his "Strong Son of God, immortal Love" and

> Ring out, wild bells, to the wild, wild sky, A
> The flying cloud, the frosty light: B
> The year is dying in the night; B
> Ring out, wild bells, and let him die. A

It takes considerable skill to rhyme all pairs of lines, and it is obviously easier to rhyme only lines two and four. Many hymn writers take the easy way out:

Not so in haste, my heart! A
Have faith in God and wait; B
Although He linger long, C
He never comes too late. B

With three-line stanzas (a tercet) all last words usually rhyme:

For all the saints who from their labors rest,
Who Thee by faith before the world confessed,
Thy Name, O Jesus, be forever blessed.

However, the "Stabat Mater" and the following are exceptions, with a rhyme scheme spread over two stanzas:

"It is finished!" Man of Sorrows! A
From Thy cross our frailty borrows A
Strength to bear and conquer thus. B

While extended there, we view Thee: C
Mighty Suff'rer, draw us to Thee, C
Sufferer victorious! B

Stanzas of more than four lines offer a wide variety of possibilities in rhyming schemes, and these will be noted under the various meters.

When only the last word is rhymed, the rhyming is called single or masculine (earth-birth; sing-King). With two syllables it is called double or feminine (singing-winging; showers-flowers). Triple rhyme involves three syllables and is rarely used (holiness-lowliness).

One additional device, called internal rhyme, should be noted. Occasionally a poet finds it possible to break up a long verse into two rhyming parts so there is an additional element of rhyme in a single line of poetry. The device is related to the limerick, where lines three and four can be considered as one long line with inner rhyme:

There was a young lady of Niger
Who smiled as she rode on a tiger.
  They returned from the ride
  With the lady inside
And the smile on the face of the tiger.

While internal rhyme is helpful to the memory it runs the danger of being flippant and light. Emily Elliott's "Thou didst leave Thy *throne* and Thy kingly *crown*" (with a false rhyme in the first line) has this stanza:

The foxes found *rest,* and the birds their *nest*
  In the shade of the forest tree;
But Thy couch was the *sod,* O Thou Son of *God,*
  In the deserts of Galilee.

While some hymn writers become too obsessed with fancy rhyming, others tend not to give enough attention to the matter. Will L. Thompson's

Softly and tenderly Jesus is calling,
  Calling for you and for me;
Patiently Jesus is waiting and watching,
  Watching for you and for me

contains no rhymes in any of the first or third lines, and lines two and four end with the word "me" in every stanza. Therefore there is not a true rhyme in the entire hymn.

Joseph Scriven's "What a Friend we have in Jesus" is little better, for the only rhymes are based on the words "bear," "where," "care," "share," "there," and "prayer"—the latter used six times.

> What a Friend we have in Jesus,
> All our sins and griefs to bear!
> What a privilege to carry
> Everything to God in prayer!
> O what peace we often forfeit,
> O what needless pain we bear,
> All because we do not carry
> Everything to God in prayer!

When a poet is more interested in form than in content, he is inclined to lavish his talents and artistry on the manipulation of words to fit a complicated pattern; the more direct his thoughts and expression, the simpler the metrical designs. The hymnal is not a book to be admired primarily for its poetry, although great hymns are always masterfully shaped as poetry. It is a book of devotion for the people, and they are the final critics.

In his "Preface to A Collection of Hymns for the Use of the People Called Methodists," 1780, John Wesley concludes with these words which put the problem in proper perspective:

That which is of infinitely more moment than the spirit of Poetry, is, the spirit of Piety. . . . It is in this view chiefly that I would recommend it to every truly pious reader, as a means of raising or quickening the spirit of devotion; of confirming his faith; of enlivening his hope; and of kindling or increasing his love to God and man. When Poetry thus keeps its place, as the handmaid of Piety, it shall attain, not a poor perishable wreath, but a crown that fadeth not away.

II. IAMBIC HYMNS

Long Meter and Variants

While many hymnals begin the metrical index by listing Short Meter hymns, from the historical viewpoint Long Meter should be studied first, for it was in this meter that Ambrose gave the church its first "modern" hymns. Iambic in form, the rhyme scheme is either AABB (rhyming couplets) or ABAB (cross rhyming). Rhyming couplets are sing-songy and tend to give a false sense of completion at the end of line two:

Again, as evening's shadow falls, A
We gather in these hallowed walls; A
And vesper hymn and vesper pray'r B
Rise mingling on the holy air. B

Cross rhyming carries the singer along with an expectancy, even a guessing, for the final two lines:

All people that on earth do dwell, A
Sing to the Lord with cheerful voice. B
Him serve with mirth, His praise forth tell; A
Come ye before Him and rejoice. B

Long meter, with eight syllables for each line of poetry, lends itself readily to majestic subjects and stately treatment. Compare the roll of the Latin hymn by Ambrose:

Splendor paternae gloriae,
De luce lucem proferens,
Lux lucis et fons luminis,
Dies diem illuminans.

with the masterly translation by Robert Bridges:

O splendor of God's glory bright,
O Thou that bringest light from light.
O Light of light, light's living spring,
O Day, all days illumining.[1]

The danger of Long Meter lies in the tendency to dullness (in 4/4 time every measure is filled to overflowing and

[1] From *The Yattendon Hymnal,* by permission of Oxford University Press.

breathing spaces are hard to find) or to pompousness. Sing through "New every morning is the love" to discover the dullness:

> New every morning is the love
> Our wak'ning and uprising prove;
> Thro' sleep and darkness safely brought,
> Restored to life and pow'r and thought

and stanza three of "Great God of nations, now to Thee" for its wordy padding:

> Here freedom spreads her banner wide
> And casts her soft and hallowed ray;
> Here Thou our fathers' steps didst guide
> In safety thro' their dangerous way.

The most successful writer in Long Meter was Isaac Watts, for a large canvas was suited to his lofty theme of God as Creator and Sovereign Lord. See:

"From all that dwell below the skies"
"High in the heav'ns, Eternal God"
"Jesus shall reign, where'er the sun"
"When I survey the wondrous cross"

John Wesley reveals mastery of the meter in his translation from Nicolaus Zinzendorf of "O Thou, to whose all-searching sight," and Charles Wesley's use can be studied in "Jesus, the sinner's Friend, to Thee":

Jesus, the sinner's Friend, to Thee,
Lost and undone, for aid I flee,
Weary of earth, myself, and sin:
Open Thine arms, and take me in.

Note particularly his division of long lines occasionally into two groups of four words. It is interesting to note that in the second stanza of "O Thou, who camest from above" Long Meter makes it possible to fit in the word "inextinguishable," which takes six of the eight possible syllables.

There let it for Thy glory burn
With inextinguishable blaze,
And trembling to its source return
In humble prayer and fervent praise.

Few modern authors have been successful in Long Meter, but two exceptions can be noted—Milton S. Littlefield's

O Son of Man, Thou madest known,
Through quiet work in shop and home,
The sacredness of common things,
The chance of life that each day brings [2]

and Frank Mason North's "Where cross the crowded ways of life," which like Charles Wesley's "O Thou, who camest from above" actually gives a sense of hurrying into the last stanza by making the last two stanzas one sentence—no small feat in this meter.

[2] From *Hymnal for Young People* (New York: Harper & Bros., 1928), used by permission.

Good LM tunes are in scarce supply. In 4/4 time all measures are filled to overflowing, and fermatas are mandatory in the middle and ending for getting a breath.

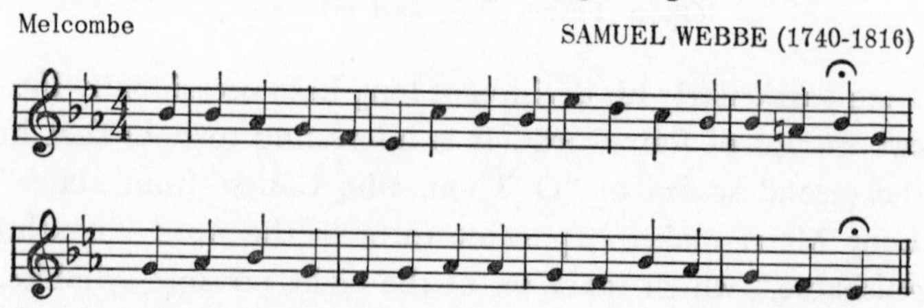

The design of "Old Hundredth" solves the problem superbly by providing rhythmic interest to offset the monotony of long lines:

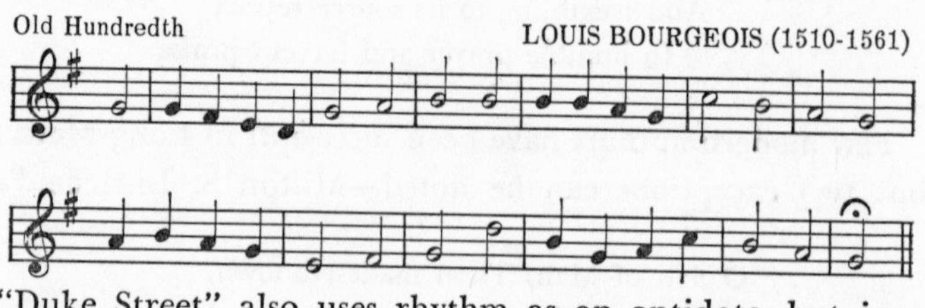

"Duke Street" also uses rhythm as an antidote, but in a different way:

"Truro," with its additional dotted notes, is a close relative:

¾ time tends to be too static for LM and is successful only to the extent that the melodic line can sustain interest. Contrast "Pentecost," with its dull repetition,

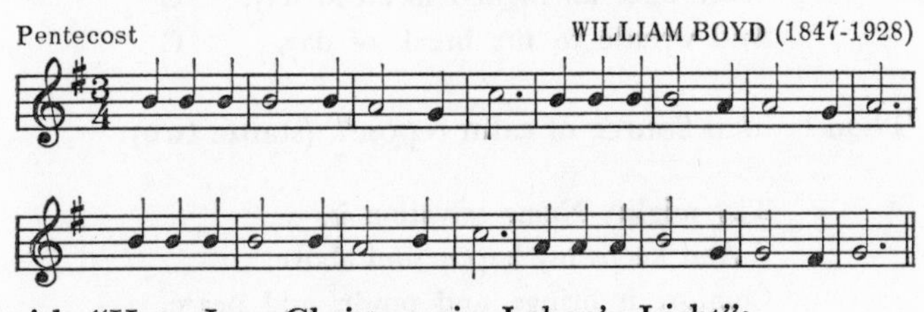

with "Herr Jesu Christ, mein Leben's Licht":

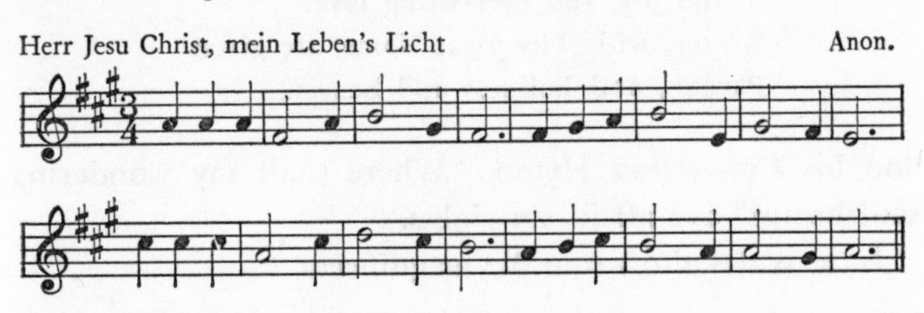

For other examples of successful LM tunes, see "Germany," "Puer Nobis Nascitur," and "Tallis' Canon."

A variant of Long Meter is six eights—88.88.88. rhyming ABABCC, or 888.888. rhyming AABCCB. John Wesley found this meter convenient for translating Paul Gerhardt's "Jesus, Thy boundless love to me" as well as Gerhard Tersteegen's "Thou hidden Love of God, whose height." Charles Wesley also found the meter to his liking and wrote over eleven hundred poems in this form. His "Wrestling Jacob" hymn

Come, O Thou Traveler unknown,	A
Whom still I hold, but cannot see;	B
My company before is gone,	A
And I am left alone with Thee:	B
With Thee all night I mean to stay,	C
And wrestle to the break of day,	C

"Thou hidden Source of calm repose" (stanza two)

Thy mighty Name salvation is,
And keeps my happy soul above:
Comfort it brings, and pow'r, and peace,
And joy, and everlasting love:
To me, with Thy great Name, are given
Pardon, and holiness and heaven,

and his Conversion Hymn, "Where shall my wondering soul begin?" are all in six eights.

Isaac Watts also wrote the magnificent

I'll praise my Maker while I've breath;	A
And when my voice is lost in death,	A

Praise shall employ my nobler powers:	B
My days of praise shall ne'er be past,	C
While life, and thought, and being last,	C
Or immortality endures	B
	(BB false rhyme)

in this design, but with AABCCB rhyme. It was undoubtedly John Wesley's favorite hymn, since he included it in all of his major collections of hymns (the first in Georgia in 1737) and sang it as he lay dying.

What is in this metrical form which so attracted evangelical poets? For one thing, it has room for arguing and for exposition. The stanza length is adequate for presentation of an idea in depth. It is interesting to note that both John Wesley in "Thou hidden Love of God, whose height"

Thou hidden Love of God, whose height,
Whose depth unfathomed, no man knows,
I see from far Thy beauteous light,
And inly sigh for Thy repose;
My heart is pained, nor can it be
At rest till it finds rest in Thee

and Charles Wesley in "Come, O Thou Traveler unknown" used the form to present a spiritual autobiography, or pilgrimage of the soul. "And can it be that I should gain" also uses the same metrical design and experential theme. See stanza two:

Long my imprisoned spirit lay,
  Fast bound in sin and nature's night;
Thine eye diffused a quickening ray,
  I woke, the dungeon flamed with light:
My chains fell off, my heart was free,
I rose, went forth, and followed Thee.

Its boldness of speech and staccato style is well worth study, and the hymn deserves wider usage.

Perhaps the problem with iambic eights is the difficulty of finding tunes which are easy for congregations to learn and sing. The characteristic problems of LM have already been mentioned, but six eights adds two more lines of full measures to compound the problem. ABABCC obviously calls for a tune in which the first two couplets are either identical or similar, with the climax and variation occurring in the last two lines. AABCCB makes for a more interesting tune since it demands more skill in melodic invention to spin out an interesting line over three phrases to the two cadences at "B" and "B." For a comparison of the two types, compare "St. Petersburg" with "Old 113th":

For an example of extreme monotony, see "Selena":

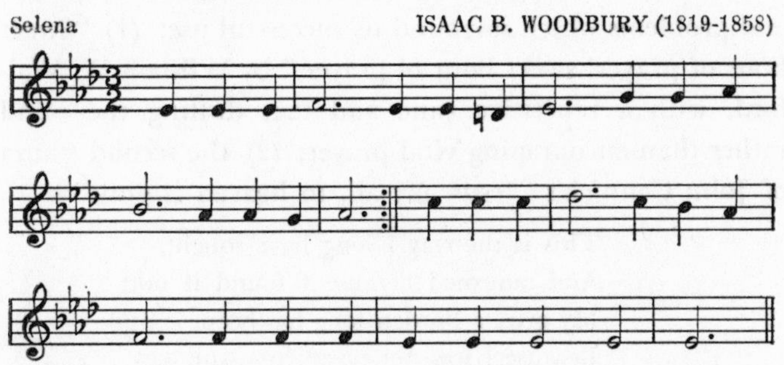

Among later writers using six eights are Frederick Faber's most successful hymn, "Faith of our fathers! living still" and Rudyard Kipling's "God of our fathers, known of old"—a prime example of the use of the meter for exposition.

Long Meter Double is just too long-winded to find much popularity with hymnal editors or congregations. For example, Joseph Addison's hymn, "The spacious firmament on high" would certainly never have achieved its popularity if there had not been an iambic arrangement made from Haydn's "The Creation" of the anapaestic chorus, "The heavens are telling the glory of God." The choral setting is decidedly superior, and the hymn tune version is effective only when sung in parts by a large congregation with good choir leadership. But aside from this, there seems to be little reason for spending so many lines of poetry to rephrase the direct language of the psalmist: "The heavens declare the glory of God, and the earth showeth forth his handiwork."

Three other examples of LMD will reveal the difficulties and problems which surround its successful use: (1) "Sweet hour of prayer! sweet hour of prayer," by William W. Walford, with a repetitive tune and text dulling the mind rather than encouraging vital prayer; (2) the second stanza of John Cennick's "Jesus, my all, to heaven is gone"

> This is the way I long have sought,
> And mourned because I found it not;
> My grief a burden long has been,
> Because I was not saved from sin.
> The more I strove against its power,
> I felt its weight and guilt the more;
> Till late I heard my Saviour say,
> "Come hither, soul, I am the way"

—a typical, tedious spiritual autobiography of the eighteenth century; and (3) Alfred Tennyson's "Ring out, wild bells, to the wild, wild sky"—with its occasional divided beats, e.g., "to the"—which is not particularly congregational in character. Needless to say, it is virtually impossible to get a really good congregational LMD tune.

Common Meter and Variants

Common Meter (86.86.) is the workhorse of hymnody. In the old English metrical psalters it was most "commonly" used for the psalm texts, since it was in reality the familiar and popular ballad meter. Common Meter Double is closer to the feel of the ballad line, which was called "fourteeners" —the sum of eight syllables in line one and six in line two, but conceived as one long flowing line. Classically the rhyme scheme is in cross lines, ABAB, but occasionally one finds a hymn which rhymes only the endings of lines two and four. Obviously, the double rhyming scheme is an additional aid to the memory and is more demanding of the poet.

With an embarrassment of riches to be found in CM listings in any hymnal, it is difficult to choose examples. However, to list the following sets a stage for comments concerning the mood of the meter:

"God moves in a mysterious way"
"The Lord's my Shepherd, I'll not want"
"O God, our help in ages past"
"Come, Holy Ghost, our hearts inspire"
"O for a heart to praise my God"
"O for a thousand tongues to sing"
"Be known to us in breaking bread"

The following characteristics of CM can be noted: the use of simple, direct words of rarely more than two syllables and mostly of one; the ease with which all hymns in this meter flow; the tendency to teach and to state facts, to be matter of fact, brief, and to the point. Even a hymn like "Come, Holy Ghost, our hearts inspire"

> Come, Holy Ghost, our hearts inspire,
> Let us Thine influence prove:
> Source of the old prophetic fire,
> Fountain of life and love,

which at first glance seems a meditative prayer, develops into a three-point exposition on the works of the Holy Spirit. Much of its strength lies in the strong accent with which each line ends. There is also a point of repose at the ends of lines two and four where the singer can gather his thoughts and breath for the next line of poetry.

Because of the imbalance of eights and sixes, 4/4 is most commonly used for CM since the dotted half note which ends phrases two and four provides the two extra pulses which make these phrases eight pulses long, balancing perfectly with the first and third which have eight syllables.

(8) (8)

"Azmon" in 3/2 solves the balance problem in a similar way by providing six basic pulses in each phrase,

but most tunes in 3/4 create a problem of imbalance in the second and fourth phrases. "St. Agnes" is typical:

There are twelve pulses in line one; but through the downbeat of measure seven the second phrase has only seven pulses. If the dotted half note is tied over for another full measure, thus providing twelve pulses, the forced balance is artificial and awkward. Many hymnal editors merely place a fermata (𝄐) over the note to indicate that a little more than three beats should be provided, but leaving the exact length of time to the organist and congregation.

Since CM is so "common," it is a treacherously and deceptively easy meter for poets to use. It rises to the heights in the hands of careful poets who know how to ring the changes of poetic devices to prevent monotony. More will be said later about some of these devices.

Even more difficult to handle without monotony or flippancy is Common Meter Double, the ballad meter. Charles Wesley almost gets a dancing movement in

> How happy every child of grace,
> Who knows his sins forgiven!
> "This earth," he cries, "is not my place,
> I seek my place in heaven:
> A country far from mortal sight,
> Which yet by faith I see,
> The land of rest, the saints' delight,
> The heaven prepared for me"

while in the hands of Washington Gladden it becomes expository in

> Behold a Sower! from afar
> He goeth forth with might;
> The rolling years His furrows are,
> His seed, the growing light;
> For all the just His word is sown,
> It springeth up alway;
> The tender blade is hope's young dawn,
> The harvest, love's new day.

Henry H. Tweedy handles the meter masterfully in

> Eternal God, whose power upholds
> Both flower and flaming star,
> To whom there is no here nor there,
> No time, no near nor far,
> No alien race, no foreign shore,

No child unsought, unknown:
O send us forth, Thy prophets true,
To make all lands Thine own!

But the longwinded, tedious tune, "Everyland," prevents the text from unfolding rapidly enough to keep the basic points clear. Perhaps the two hymns closest to the folksiness of CMD are "It came upon the midnight clear" and

O Master Workman of the race,
Thou Man of Galilee,
Who with the eyes of early youth
Eternal things did see:
We thank Thee for Thy boyhood faith
That shone Thy whole life through;
"Did ye not know it is my work
My Father's work to do?"

CMD can be used for strong texts if the tune is strong, e.g., "Llangloffan."

Phillips Brooks uses a slight variation of CMD (86.86.76.86.) in "O little town of Bethlehem." It is mentioned here, however, for its use of inner rhyme in lines three and seven:

Above thy *deep* and dreamless *sleep*
The hopes and *fears* of all the *years.*

Where Brooks is successful, a lesser poet would be in danger of flippancy created by the ballad meter and limerick style inner rhyme.

Closely related to CMD is 76.76.D. which in a sense is an effeminization of the more virile form. Many CMD tunes fit 76.76.D. equally well because both have a folksy, free flowing style. Instead of ending lines two and four with a strong beat, the last syllable is a falling one with the accent of CM missing:

CM / ∪ /
76. / ∪

The result is a necessity for double rhyming the last two syllables and using multisyllabled words. The rhymes tend to be more obvious, particularly when the same rhyme is used for three stanzas as in the case of "The Church's one foundation": foundation, creation, nation, salvation, tribulation, consummation.

Here are the rhymes in James Montgomery's excellent 76.76.D. hymn, "Hail, to the Lord's Anointed":

Anointed-appointed
speedy-needy
showers-flowers
oppression-transgression
sighing-dying
mountains-fountains
never-ever

The danger of 76.76.D. is that the meter lends itself all too readily to facile writing and composing. Gilbert K. Chesterton, whose hymn "O God of earth and altar" is about as far removed from the usual easygoing style of the meter as any author has gone, chose the meter because he thought "Aurelia" was the "typical tune for hymns."

Yet for all the dangers inherent in its structure, it has framed the following masterpieces: "All glory, laud, and honor," "O Sacred Head, now wounded," "God is my strong salvation," "Lead on, O King Eternal," and "The voice of God is calling."

Short Meter

Short meter, once called the poulter's measure because of his custom of giving twelve eggs for the first dozen and thirteen or fourteen for the second dozen, is made up of two couplets—the first containing twelve syllables and the second fourteen.

∪/∪/∪/ ∪/∪/∪/

∪/∪/∪/∪/ ∪/∪/∪/

Of the three chief patterns of the English psalters (CM, LM, and SM) it stands last in percentage of use; an examination of its design quickly reveals the reason. In the first line of poetry there are only six syllables available, giving no room for wordiness. The author must get his message across in the first line, knowing that he can reinforce it in the second, then develop it further in the last fourteen syllables. Notice the use of strong, simple words in James Montgomery's hymn:

Stand up, and bless the Lord,
Ye people of His choice;
Stand up, and bless the Lord your God
With heart and soul and voice.

A random sampling of opening lines reveals the following terse beginnings:

"A charge to keep I have"
"Blest be the tie that binds"
"Rise up, O men of God"
"I love Thy kingdom, Lord"
"Come, sound His praise abroad"

It might be called the exhorting meter, for its abrupt, direct opening line attracts attention. Its ecstatic nature is revealed in the double form (SMD) as used by Charles Wesley in "Servant of God, well done!" with its opening third stanza, "O happy, happy soul!" (The hymn originally was SMD but is divided into four SM stanzas in the 1935 edition of *The Methodist Hymnal.*) Cross rhyming (ABAB) is the accepted pattern, but occasionally rhymes will be limited to the second and fourth lines.

SMD was a favorite of Charles Wesley, and half of the hymns in this meter in *The Methodist Hymnal* are by him. "Soldiers of Christ, arise" is an excellent exhorting hymn, and shares the same tune ("Diademata") with a text by Matthew Bridges,

Crown Him with many crowns,
The Lamb upon His throne;

Hark! how the heavenly anthem drowns
All music but its own!
Awake, my soul, and sing
Of Him who died for thee,
And hail Him as thy matchless King
Through all eternity

revealing uniquely both the exhorting and ecstatic natures of the meter. George Matheson's

Make me a captive, Lord,
And then I shall be free;
Force me to render up my sword,
And I shall conqueror be.
I sink in life's alarms
When by myself I stand;
Imprison me within Thine arms,
And strong shall be my hand

deserves careful study for its skilful handling of the meter and its unsurpassed use of paradox.

8's and 6's

There are many ways to combine sixes and eights in addition to the three basic Short, Common, and Long meters; while some pose problems in musical settings, they all have a refreshingly "unsquare" feeling. At one time they were called PM (Peculiar or Particular Meter) to distinguish them from the three basic iambic forms. The first is 66.66.88., known as HM, or Hallelujah Meter, with a usual rhyme scheme of ABABCC. One interesting rhyming variation is found in Samuel Crossman's (1624-1684) "My song is love unknown," in which the last two lines are really four groups of four with cross rhyme:

O who am I
  That for my sake
  My Lord should take
Frail flesh, and die?

Watts builds with strong words through the first four lines, then spills over into the longer group of eights in

The Lord Jehovah reigns,
  His throne is built on high;
The garments He assumes
  Are light and majesty;
His glories shine with beams so bright
No mortal eye can bear the sight.

Charles Wesley's masterpiece,

Rejoice, the Lord is King:
  Your Lord and King adore!
Rejoice, give thanks, and sing,
  And triumph evermore:
Lift up your heart, lift up your voice!
Rejoice, again I say, rejoice!

uses the short six syllables for imperative exhortations as he did in SMD. "Darwall's 148th," one of the very best tunes in this meter, is a perfect match for the text and makes an excellent alternate tune for "The Lord Jehovah reigns." The tune "Lenox"

is a roughhewn early American tune which matches the clarion quality of

> Blow ye the trumpet, blow!
> The gladly solemn sound
> Let all the nations know,
> To earth's remotest bound,
> The year of jubilee is come!
> Return, ye ransomed sinners, home

by Charles Wesley.

F. Bland Tucker, translator and poet who helped edit *The Hymnal 1940,* has extended the form to 66.66.888. in a hymn for the family:

Our Father, by whose Name
All fatherhood is known,
Who dost in love proclaim
Each family thine own,
Bless thou all parents, guarding well,
With constant love as sentinel,
The homes in which thy people dwell.[3]

It is usually sung to the Welsh tune "Rhosymedre," one of the few available in this extended meter.

Two other modern poets have contributed a variation on CM by adding two more lines, making 86.86.86. with only the sixes rhyming, ABCBDB. One is

Awake, awake to love and work,
The lark is in the sky,
The fields are wet with diamond dew,
The worlds awake to cry
Their blessings on the Lord of Life,
As He goes meekly by [4]

by Geoffrey A. Studdert-Kennedy, and the other is

O holy city, seen of John,
Where Christ, the Lamb, doth reign,
Within whose four-square walls shall come
No night, nor need, nor pain,

[3] By permission of The Church Pension Fund.

[4] From *The Unutterable Beauty* (London: Hodder and Stoughton; New York: Harper & Row). Used by permission.

And where the tears are wiped from eyes
  That shall not weep again

by Walter Russell Bowie. Both are excellent hymns, and both have social implications although their themes are poles apart.

Another variation which combines Common and Long Meter is 86.86.88. by Samuel Longfellow,

I look to Thee in every need,
  And never look in vain;
I feel Thy strong and tender love,
  And all is well again:
The thought of Thee is mightier far
Than sin and pain and sorrow are.

The hymn is not completely successful for two reasons. While there are two ideas set forth, man's need and God's faithfulness in providing for our needs, they are not presented in the framework of the meter, i.e., the first four lines of 86.86. could better be balanced by the last two lines of 88., each presenting a different side of the theme. Second, cross rhyming would have helped to move the poem along more smoothly, but the singer must go too far before he finds the first two rhymes, and then is aware of the sudden appearance of couplet rhyming in lines five and six. The attractive tune, "O Jesu," has helped keep the text in circulation.

Two extensions of CM can be found which involve the third line of eight syllables. One is John Greenleaf Whittier's "Dear Lord and Father of mankind" which is 86.886. Lengthening the poem by eight syllables before the quiet closing six gives the effect of a gentle sigh, of a prayer rising fervently and then falling in perfect submission. The rhyme scheme is also notable, ABAAB, and pushes the mind on to the end without complexity or distraction. The other extension is found in a text by Thomas T. Lynch in 86.86.888.6. and a rhyme scheme of ABCBDDDB. Set to a traditional Swiss melody it has all of the robustness of folk music, and can be considered one of the devil's tunes which the church has snatched for holier use:

My faith, it is an oaken staff,
The traveler's well-loved aid;
My faith, it is a weapon stout,
The soldier's trusty blade:
I'll travel on, and still be stirred
By silent thought or social word;
By all my perils undeterred,
A soldier-pilgrim staid.

Another extension, that of LM, is found in George Matheson's familiar hymn,

O Love that wilt not let me go,	A
I rest my weary soul in Thee;	B
I give Thee back the life I owe,	A
That in Thine ocean depths its flow	A
May richer, fuller be	B

with a simple and effective rhyme scheme. It is actually LM with an added six syllables, 88.88.6. Its effect is that of struggling for four lines, then yielding at last in quiet confidence.

An abbreviation of LM is found in 888.4., generally an unsatisfying meter to sing. There are no really fine hymns available, but "For all the blessings of the year" and "O Lord of heaven and earth and sea" are the least objectionable. The problem lies in the last line of only four syllables —too short to bring the thought to final focus or a strong finish. For instance, it is hard to keep a straight face when singing the second stanza of Harriet Auber's "Our blest Redeemer, ere He breathed," although the poem has excellence up to the point of the last phrase of the second stanza:

> He came in tongues of living flame,
> To teach, convince, subdue:
> All-powerful as the wind He came,
> As viewless, too.

Another variation is 88.86. or 888.6., an improvement over 888.4. Examples are

> It fell upon a summer day,
> When Jesus walked in Galilee,
> The mothers from a village brought
> Their children to His knee [5]

and

[5] Used by permission of Henry Brooke.

O Holy Saviour, Friend unseen,
Since on Thine arm Thou bidd'st me lean,
Help me, throughout life's changing scene,
  By faith to cling to Thee.

The first rhymes lines two and four; the second uses AAAB. Technically, "Just as I am, without one plea" is 888.6. with an AAAB rhyme, but the tune "Woodworth," being LM, calls for a repetition of the text, "I come," to fill out the tune. The hymn would be far stronger without the repeated words, for six words better denote complete surrender of the singer in spite of all the reasons that can be found to resist the claim of God.

One of the classic variants is 886.886., a design which is unfortunately destroyed or hidden by the tune "Ariel" to which all three examples in *The Methodist Hymnal* are set. In the hands of Watts and Wesley the meter is a series of magnificent arches. The rhyme scheme is AABCCB. An example is stanza two of "Let all on earth their voices raise."

He framed the globe; He built the sky;
He made the shining worlds on high,
  And reigns in glory there:
His beams are majesty and light;
His beauties, how divinely bright!
  His dwelling place, how fair!

It is senseless to repeat the last line, particularly to a musical phrase (in "Ariel") which in rhythm and descending pitch destroys the glorious ending. That Charles Wesley felt this meter was an effective means of ecstatic utterance is clear from reading

> O Love divine, how sweet Thou art!
> When shall I find my willing heart
>   All taken up by Thee?
> I thirst, I faint, I die to prove
> The greatness of redeeming love,
>   The love of Christ to me

and his marvelous invitation to earthbound man to behold "The Beatific Sight":

> Come on, my Partners in distress,
> My comrades thro' the wilderness
>   Who still your bodies feel,
> A while forget your griefs, and fears,
> And look beyond the vale of tears
>   To that celestial hill.
>
> Beyond the bounds of time, and space,
> Look forward to that happy place,
>   The saints' secure abode,
> On faith's strong eagle pinions rise,
> And force your passage to the skies,
>   And scale the Mount of God.
>
> (From *Hymns and Sacred Poems,* 1739)

This meter, the old romance meter, was Charles Wesley's second most favorite (following 88.88.88.) with nine hundred poems. It is much lighter in texture, less argumentative or didactic, and tends to carry the reader along with a sense of boundless energy and enthusiasm. Perhaps modern day Christians no longer have this kind of joy, for some of the contemporary hymnals do not include the meter at all.

One final group of 8's should be listed—8 8 8. with Alleluias. "The strife is o'er, the battle done" is an iambic text set to a tune with a trochaic beginning (or to be specific, a dactylic first measure). It has been criticized as a poor hymn which has ridden to success on the coattails of a fine tune. But the form must be popular, for *The Pilgrim Hymnal* includes three other examples: the classic

O sons and daughters, let us sing!
The King of heaven, the glorious King,
O'er death today rose triumphing.
Alleluia!

Cyril A. Alington's contemporary

Good Christian men rejoice and sing!
Now is the triumph of our King!
To all the world glad news we bring:
Alleluia!

and Frederick L. Hosmer's Unitarian funeral hymn,

O Lord of life, wher'er they be
Safe in Thine own eternity,
Our dead are living unto Thee:
Alleluia! *

* Used by permission of The Beacon Press.

Other Iambic Meters

Frank Baker says that "Charles Wesley wrote in no fewer than 45 iambic metres, and in each of 15 of them wrote over a thousand lines of verse." [7] To chase down all these would be pointless and fruitless, but there are several fairly frequent uses of iambic which must be noted.

The first has to do with groupings of sixes and fours, which can also be considered as long lines of tens. The most familiar example is "I need Thee every hour." The rhyming occurs only at the ends of lines two and four. The short lines are almost gasps, as if the poet were expressing need, even to the uttermost.

I need Thee every hour,
  Most gracious Lord;
No tender voice like Thine
  Can peace afford.

Robert Lowry's tune, with refrain, spoils the effectiveness of the meter. *The Hymnal 1940* has a short tune, without refrain, called "Frogmore" (or "Parratt") which brings out the best qualities of the text.

[7] *Representative Verse of Charles Wesley* (Nashville: Abingdon Press, 1962), p. xliv.

Four sixes (66.66.) and 66.66.D. can be either iambic or trochaic, but are flimsy meters because of the shortness of all lines and the monotony of rhythm which develops over several stanzas. *The Pilgrim Hymnal* has only one example, "Thy kingdom come, O Lord" by Frederick L. Hosmer, definitely not one of his best moments; and *The Methodist Hymnal* has one example in each pattern: the too carefully contrived

> Not so in haste, my heart!
> Have faith in God and wait;
> Although He linger long,
> He never comes too late.
>
> He never cometh late;
> He knoweth what is best;
> Vex not thyself in vain;
> Until He cometh, rest

and the much better

> My Jesus, as Thou wilt!
> O may Thy will be mine!
> Into Thy hand of love
> I would my all resign.
> Through sorrow or thro' joy,
> Conduct me as Thine own;
> And help me still to say,
> "My Lord, Thy will be done"

of Benjamin Schmolck, miserably set to Weber's "Jewett." "Laudes Domini," also from the German, uses 666.666.

successfully in "When morning gilds the skies." The rhyme scheme of AABCCB is helpful in sustaining interest, and the tune by Joseph Barnby is certainly one of his more successful.

The unusual iambic pattern of 67.67.66.66. was used by Martin Rinkart for "Now thank we all our God." The short lines seem adequate to modern ears unfortunately accustomed to halting at the ends of all chorale lines. Written as a table grace, the short lines are easy for children to remember and to sing. George W. Briggs has written a modern masterpiece in the same meter,

> Christ is the world's true light,
> Its captain of salvation,
> The daystar clear and bright
> Of every man and nation;
> New life, new hope awakes,
> Where'er men own his sway:
> Freedom her bondage breaks,
> And night is turned to day [8]

set to another German tune, "O Gott, du frommer Gott."

Another unusual iambic form, more exciting to sing because of its division of twelve syllables into different patterns, is 66.84.D. It was used both by Thomas Olivers in the eighteenth century and by Max Landsberg and Newton Mann in the nineteenth for their translations of the Jewish Doxology, "The God of Abraham praise."

[8] From *Songs of Praise, Enlarged Edition,* © 1931, renewed 1959, by permission of Oxford University Press.

The God of Abraham praise,
All praised be His Name,
Who was, and is, and is to be,
And still the same!
The one eternal God,
Ere aught that now appears;
The first, the Last: beyond all thought
His timeless years.

The third and seventh phrases (of eight syllables) provide adequate space for the thoughts to gather momentum and to end in climactic and compact four-syllabled ideas. The Wesleys must have enjoyed the hymn as much for its rhythm as for its content.

8 7.8 7. and 10's

In much the same way that 76.76.D. is created by dropping one syllable from lines one and three of CM, 87.87. is created by adding one syllable to lines two and four.

The King of love my Shepherd is, (8)
Whose goodness faileth never; (7)
I nothing lack if I am His (8)
And He is mine forever. (7)

Like its sister form, it is gentler and less virile that CM because of its falling, yielding cadence and double syllable rhyming. It has been used sparsely. Note the rhymes: never-ever, leadeth-feedeth, sought me-brought me, beside me-guide me, never-ever. The result is one of sweetness rather than strength. It is well worth while to compare Baker's version of the Psalm with that of the Scottish Psalter

> The Lord's my Shepherd, I'll not want;
> He makes me down to lie
> In pastures green; He leadeth me
> The quiet waters by

or with that of George Herbert (from whom Baker recast his version):

> The God of love my Shepherd is
> And He that doth me feed;
> While He is mine, and I am His,
> What can I want or need?
> (From *Songs of Praise*)

One other fine text in this meter is

> Strengthen for service, Lord, the hands
> That holy things have taken;
> Let ears that now have heard Thy songs
> To clamor never waken [9]

a translation and paraphrase of a communion prayer in the Liturgy of Malabar, the fifth-century Nestorian rite in South India. While an occasional iambic hymn may be found in 87.87.D., its brother meter in trochaic (see p. 72) is more effective and more widely used.

A typically German iambic meter is 87.87.887., a form which like so much of the German material can be classi-

[9] From *The English Hymnal* by permission of Oxford University Press.

fied as unsquare or asymetrical, in contrast to the usual balance of English hymnody. An excellent example of skilful work in the meter is

Sing praise to God who reigns above,
  The God of all creation,
The God of power, the God of love,
  The God of our salvation;
With healing balm my soul He fills,
And every faithless murmur stills:
  To God all praise and glory.

The first four lines are of a good length for exposition, and the next two become the development section, ending with an ascription of praise drawn from the opening phrase. The tune "Mit Freuden Zart" is a masterpiece of construction with its use of balanced phrases, repetition, and development. The rhyme scheme is effective: ABABCCD. Another example of the same form is the less well known

We come unto our fathers' God,
  Their Rock is our salvation;
Th'eternal arms, their dear abode,
  We make our habitation.
We bring Thee, Lord, the praise they brought,
We seek Thee as Thy saints have sought
  In every generation

written by Thomas H. Gill, an Englishman, but sung to the German "Nun freut euch."

Another German masterpiece with an uneven number

of phrases is "A mighty fortress is our God" with a total of nine phrases: 87.87.66.667., with rhyme scheme ABABCCDDE. While some hymnals use a fermata between the 8's and 7's, a study of the music and the text indicates that there is only one musical phrase and one long textual idea running for fifteen syllables before a point of rest is reached. The first two groups of fifteen are the exposition of the main idea, and the remaining short phrases are defiant short jabs, ending with a good uppercut seven (if a boxing figure of speech is not too farfetched!)

10 10. 10 10. can well be called the meter of the nineteenth century, for almost every example in *The Methodist Hymnal* was written in that era. Very few are excellent hymns, and most sound like poems, set to tunes as an afterthought. While Charles Wesley wrote many poems in decasyllabic lines, he did not use the meter for hymnody. The lines are long, the thought process becomes too involved, and the mind has wandered long before it arrives at the end of a stanza. Couplet rhyming, AABB, is much more common than ABAB, and is preferable since the length of the lines makes it virtually impossible for the mind to recall any rhymes too far apart. The two most familiar hymns in the meter are "Abide with me: fast falls the eventide" and "Here, O my Lord, I see Thee face to face."

An interesting variant is 10 10.

> Peace, perfect peace, in this dark world of sin?
> The blood of Jesus whispers peace within.

Here the meter seems correct, for the first line is broken into two groups (four and six) to ask the question; then the answer is given in a long sweep of ten syllables. Another interesting variant is this 10 10. 10 10. 10. by Clifford Bax:

> Turn back, O man, forswear thy foolish ways.
> Old now is earth, and none may count her days,
> Yet thou, her child, whose head is crowned with flame,
> Still wilt not hear thine inner God proclaim:
> "Turn back, O man, forswear thy foolish ways" [10]

sung to the magnificent "Old 124th" from the Genevan Psalter. Still another variant is six tens, which is pushing the limit precariously. "Be still, my soul, the Lord is on thy side" is quite wearisome when sung to "Finlandia" since the rhythm of the music and words are at constant odds. One is constantly aware of holding on inordinately long to peculiar syllables (ly, fu-, te-, con-); to parody the Psalm verse, "My mouth shall be filled with odd syllables." The most successful hymn in six tens is John Byrom's hymn-poem written as a Christmas present for his daughter:

> Christians, awake! salute the happy morn
> Whereon the Saviour of the world was born;
> Rise to adore the mystery of love,
> Which hosts of angels chanted from above;
> With them the joyful tidings first begun
> Of God Incarnate and the Virgin's Son.

[10] Used by permission of A. D. Peters & Co.

Only one classic hymn related to 10's is included in *The Methodist Hymnal,* and it is George Herbert's "Let all the world in every corner sing," which John Wesley included in his hymn collections.

Let all the world in every corner sing:
My God and King!
The heavens are not too high,
His praise may thither fly;
The earth is not too low,
His praises there may grow.
Let all the world in every corner sing:
My God and King!

The meter is 10 4. 66. 66. 10 4., perfect for the ideas Herbert is expressing, and the rhyme scheme (AABBCCAA), which is not bothered by the uneven phrase lengths, rolls matters along in fine style. Many composers have been attracted to the text, and every hymnal seems to try a different setting. Robert Guy McCutchan's "All the World," while perhaps too sequential, has a gay child-like quality which fits the text.

One final iambic pattern is 11 10. 11 10., related to four 10's but with a feminine ending for lines one and three. The same problems noted for 10's apply here. "Still, still with Thee, when purple morning breaketh" is satisfactory as devotional poetry but poor for singing, particularly with Mendelssohn's piano piece "without words," "Consolation." Whittier's "O brother man, fold to thy heart thy brother" is primarily a poem which is skilfully set as an anthem called "Worship" by Geoffrey Shaw (Novello). As a hymn, it is difficult to set to a congregational tune since ideas and phrases tend to move irregularly past normal breathing spots. The wedding hymn, "O perfect Love, all human thoughts transcending," is fairly successful in the meter, but it is usually sung as a solo. The only example which has had wide usage is "Ancient of Days, who sittest throned in glory"—a tedious Trinitarian hymn with too many stanzas, too much forced imagery, too obvious an outline, and for a tune a dreadful pseudo-march, "Ancient of Days," atrociously harmonized. And so, having pushed iambic hymnody to and beyond the limits of usefulness, we turn now to trochaic forms.

III. TROCHAIC HYMNS

If the discussion of iambic meters has been long, it was demanded by the large body of hymns created in the meter of the rising foot (∪/). Now we turn to the meter of the falling foot (/∪). The trochaic form does not wear as well as iambic because it gives impact immediately, then fades away. Iambic is always urging the sound and sense onward to a final strong point of accent and thought. Trochaic is abrupt; it comes to the point immediately. It commands attention; it is decisive.

The first trochaic meter commonly found in the metrical index is 65.65. or 65.65.D.

> Now the day is over,
> Night is drawing nigh,
> Shadows of the evening
> Steal across the sky.

Read this well-known example aloud as a poem and notice how frustrating it is to be stopped so soon after starting a line of poetry. Sabine Baring-Gould, the author, wrote a tune for his own text called "Eudoxia,"

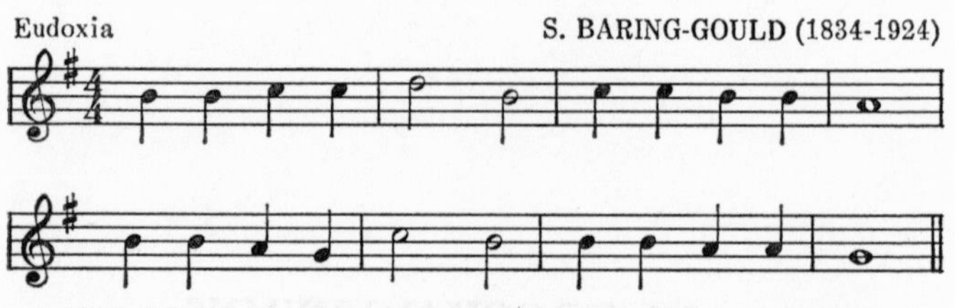

Copyright by J. Curwen & Sons, Ltd. Used by permission.

but it is quite obvious why Barnby's "Merrial" is used instead. "Eudoxia" quits musically at the end of every two measures; "Merrial" sustains musical interest by giving the basses and tenors melodic material where interest is most apt to lag.

Sullivan also succeeded in hiding the monotony of the fundamental

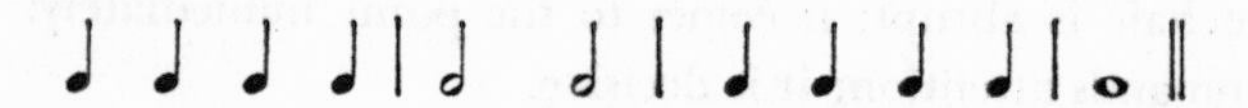

inherent in this meter in "St. Gertrude" for "Onward, Christian soldiers." Trochaic suits the imperative "Onward," and there is a sense of urgency in the meter. In contrast look at

Brightly gleams our banner,
Pointing to the sky,
Waving on Christ's soldiers
To their home on high.
Marching thro' the desert,
Gladly thus we pray,
Still with hearts united,
Singing on our way

which is sing-songy. The short lines sound as if they are being written down to children, yet with an adult imperative pushiness. Aside from the impossible ideas of the text, the meter is a poor choice.

John Ellerton's translation from Fortunatus represents another poor choice of meter:

"Welcome, happy morning;"
Age to age shall say:
"Hell today is vanquished,
Heaven is won today."
Lo! the dead is living,
God for ever more:
Him, their true Creator,
All His works adore.

Trochaic movement? Excellent! Short lines of 6's and 5's? No. The start and stop movement stifles the enthusiasm and joy of Easter, and nothing can keep the tune "Hermas" interesting.

Sevens

In a sense, 77.77. can be considered a variant of Common Meter, if one syllable is removed from the start of line one and added at the start of the second.

∪/∪/∪/∪/ /∪/∪/∪/

∪/∪/∪/ /∪/∪/∪/

Or it can be considered a variant of Long Meter, with the upbeat omitted.

(∪)/∪/∪/∪/

77.77. is by far the most common and useful trochaic pattern, and, as indicated in the introduction, Charles Wesley used it effectively for his Easter hymn, "Christ the Lord is risen today." With seven syllables he had working room to express ideas adequately while retaining the terseness of short lines and strong downbeats. Note the strong beginning words: Christ, Lives, Love's, Soar, Sons, Where, Fought, Raise, Once, Death, Made, Sing.

Four sevens is a treacherous meter for it can be written facilely, and rhymes tend to be oppressively obvious (usually cross rhymed ABAB). First, consider Elizabeth R. Charles' poor choice of meter and its use in the following:

> Never further than Thy cross,
> Never higher than Thy feet;
> Here earth's precious things seem dross,
> Here earth's bitter things grow sweet.

There is nothing meditative about trochaic movement, yet this is meant to be a meditative hymn. Through the entire hymn there are many weak words accented as opening syllables. The rhyme of "dross" and "cross," bad enough, is made obvious by the short lines. Contrast this with Samuel Longfellow's

> Holy Spirit, Truth Divine,
> Dawn upon this soul of mine;
> Word of God, and inward Light,
> Wake my spirit, clear my sight.

As a means of invoking the Spirit of God, trochaic imperatives are excellent. Other words which start lines are: Love, Power, Right, Glow, Fill, King, Kindle, Perish, Bravely, Firmly. Here is fine use of meter and matter.

77.77.77. and 77.77.D. are more popular forms, even though the double form creates problems in avoiding monotony in rhythm and melody. Toplady's "Rock of Ages, cleft for me" is a fine example of six sevens which has been imitated by later writers with less skill, e.g., "Jesus, Saviour, pilot me." Wesley's

Christ, whose glory fills the skies,
  Christ, the true, the only Light,
Sun of righteousness, arise,
  Triumph o'er the shades of night;
Day-Spring from on high, be near;
Day-Star, in my heart appear

combines strong opening words with use of antithesis (light and dark) to form an excellent hymn. Among 77.77.D. examples, Charles Wesley's

Jesus, Lover of my soul,
  Let me to Thy bosom fly,
While the nearer waters roll,
  While the tempest still is high:
Hide me, O my Saviour, hide,
  Till the storm of life is past;
Safe into the haven guide;
  O receive my soul at last

is monumental in its balance of God's strength and man's sense of need in times of temptation. What might have been a disastrous choice in meter proves to be a strength. Another fascinating use of four sevens double is found in

Sinners, turn: why will ye die?
God, your Maker, asks you why;
God, who did your being give,
Made you with Himself to live;
He the fatal cause demands,
Asks the work of His own hands:

Why, ye thankless creatures, why
Will ye cross His love, and die?

Contrast this text and meter with the bouncy dactyls of

Rescue the perishing,
Care for the dying,
Snatch them in pity from sin and the grave;
Weep o'er the erring one,
Lift up the fallen,
Tell them of Jesus the mighty to save

as a poor means of expressing concern for the souls of the unsaved. Wesley uses all sorts of poetic devices to get the message across. Note the balance of "Sinners" and "God" in the first lines. Note the Trinitarian formula: "God your Maker—Saviour—(the) Spirit." Note in line two: God-Made; God-Died; He-Wooed; line three: He-Asks. And finally the emphasis on the words "why" and "will." More will be said about poetic devices later, but in this hymn they fit uniquely into the trochaic design.

There are a few examples of 76.76.D. which are trochaic rather than the more usual iambic.

Iambic: ∪/∪/∪/∪ ∪/∪/∪/
Trochaic: /∪/∪/∪/ /∪/∪/∪

While there is strength and directness, the final six in each line ends on a weak pulse and adds a touch of gentleness. A fine example is

Gentle Mary laid her Child
  Lowly in a manger;
There He lay, the undefiled,
  To the world a Stranger.
Such a Babe in such a place,
  Can He be the Saviour?
Ask the saved of all the race
  Who have found His favor [1]

set to the fourteenth century spring carol, "Tempus Adest Floridum." Needless to say, this tune will not fit any of the usual iambic 76.76.D. texts, such as "The Church's one foundation."

An interesting variation of six sevens is found in 78.78. 88. The tune "Liebster Jesu" is commonly used for texts in this meter, and is found in *The Methodist Hymnal.* Again, the feminine endings of the 8's tend to soften the effect of the trochaic beginnings, and the two-syllabled rhymes are more difficult to handle. In "Blessed Jesus, at Thy word" the rhymes are: hear Thee-fear Thee; holy-solely; shrouded-clouded; win us-within us; etc. Percy Dearmer's

Book of books, our people's strength,
  Statesman's, teacher's, hero's treasure,
Bringing freedom, spreading truth,
  Shedding light that none can measure:
Wisdom comes to those who know thee,
All the best we have we owe thee [2]

[1] Used by permission of Alta Lind Cook.

[2] From *Songs of Praise, Enlarged Edition,* © 1931, renewed 1959, by permission of Oxford University Press.

is particularly fine in its direct, forceful, and vivid language, and is perhaps his finest hymn.

The trochaic pattern seems to invite unusual metrical designs with use of inner rhyming. Three examples will suffice, two of them German:

847.D.

Come, my soul, thou must be waking;
Now is breaking
O'er the earth another day:
Come to Him who made this splendor;
See thou render
All thy feeble strength can pay.

8336.D. (or 866.D)

All my heart this night rejoices,
As I hear, Far and near,
Sweetest angel voices;
"Christ is born," their choirs are singing,
Till the air, Everywhere,
Now with joy is ringing.

85.85.843.

Angel voices, ever singing
Round Thy throne of light,
Angel harps forever ringing,
Rest not day nor night;
Thousands only live to bless Thee,
And confess Thee
Lord of might.

The last example also has the distinction of being one of the rare hymns in which a single word fills up an entire line of poetry, the final "3" of stanza four consisting of the word "Melody." In all of these examples there is a sense of exuberance and joy, and a sense of rightness in accent as well as rhyme.

8 7.8 7. and 8 7.8 7.D.

Whereas iambic eights start with a preparatory upbeat, trochaic eights begin with an accent and fill up whole measures of 4/4 time.

4/4 / ◡ / ◡ | / ◡ / ◡ |

Coupled with a seven, which ends on a strong pulse, trochaic 87.87. is an excellent pattern for texts requiring large scope yet calling for strength. Texts such as

God is love: His mercy brightens
All the path in which we rove;
Bliss He wakes and woe He lightens:
God is wisdom, God is love

and

For the bread, which Thou hast broken;
For the wine, which Thou hast poured;
For the words, which Thou hast spoken;
Now we give Thee thanks, O Lord[3]

[3] By permission of Barbara Benson Jefferys.

are fine examples. Where iambic 87.87. calls for a two-syllable rhyme at the ends of lines two and four, trochaic 87.87. demands two-syllable rhyme at the ends of lines one and three. The result is strength at the end of the middle and close of the hymn where strength is desirable. Compare the second stanza of "The King of love my Shepherd is":

87.87. Iambic

Where streams of living water flow,
  My ransomed soul He leadeth,
And, where the verdant pastures grow,
  With food celestial feedeth

with

87.87. Trochaic

May the grace of Christ our Saviour,
  And the Father's boundless love,
With the Holy Spirit's favor
  Rest upon us from above.

87.87.D. has been used for some of our most popular hymns, as the following representative list shows:

"Come, Thou Fount of every blessing"
"Come, thou long-expected Jesus"
"Glorious things of thee are spoken"
"Jesus spreads his banner o'er us"
"Joyful, joyful, we adore Thee"
"Love divine, all loves excelling"
"Not alone for mighty empire"
"Once to every man and nation"
"Praise the Lord! ye heavens adore Him"

While subject matter is varied, there is grandeur in all these hymns indicative of the strength of the meter and its ability to carry massive ideas in its fifteen syllables per double line.

A variant of 8's and 7's is 87.87.87., with the same general characteristics of strength. The following are typical:

"Angels from the realms of glory"
"God of grace and God of glory"
"Guide me, O Thou great Jehovah"
"Let all mortal flesh keep silence"
"Look, ye saints! the sight is glorious"
"Praise, my soul, the King of heaven"

With the exception of "Let all mortal flesh keep silence," all the other hymns could be accurately listed as 87.87.47., with the four doubled by repeating a word or phrase, such as "Come and worship," "Grant us wisdom, grant us courage," "Bread of heaven," "Crown Him! Crown Him!" and "Alleluia." The rhyme scheme ABABCB coupled with a tune which repeats the major theme in the second phrase and uses the third phrase for climax, gives a powerful boost to congregational singing. "Cwm Rhondda" and "Regent Square" invite enthusiastic participation; many fine Welsh tunes are cast in this form.

Because of the direct and terse nature of trochaics, few hymns are found with longer lines than 8's and 7's. Where poets wish to cover ground rapidly, the movement must lighten. So they turn naturally to dactylic and anapaestic.

IV. DACTYLIC AND ANAPAESTIC

Pure dactylic verse (/⌣⌣) is most rare because it is dependent on word forms which are primarily found in Latin. The opening line of Bernard of Cluny's *De Contemptu Mundi,* ca. 1145, *"Hora novissima, tempora pessima sunt: vigilemus"* is only one of nearly three thousand lines in this galloping meter.

While its sister meter, the anapaest, is a classic poetic foot (⌣⌣/), prior to the time of Charles Wesley it was not thought to be sufficiently respectable for church use. In England it was the basis for a tripping ballad form, and was also used for satirical poetry. Frank Baker says, "Wesley's popularization of the anapaest in his hymns seems to have been at least as important in improving its status as the somewhat hesitant use made of it by secular poets, and he was a pioneer in making it the medium for the irrepressible lilt of emotions which burst the bonds of conventional verse, as they did of conventional religion. If not responsible for its introduction, it fell to his lot to bring it under firmer discipline, and to train it for unaccustomed tasks." [1]

Wesley's first experiments were with 55.55.65.65. with cross rhyming, and it became a favorite form. Probably influenced by tunes like "Hanover" and "Lyons," it was easy for Wesley to dash off:

Ye servants of God,
  Your Master proclaim,
And publish abroad
  His wonderful Name;
The Name all-victorious
  Of Jesus extol;
His kingdom is glorious,
  And rules over all.

The rhythm is infectious, and the mind is thrust forward through the short phrases. The inner rhymes (if two lines are taken together as units) help the memory. In the

[1] *Op. cit.,* p. xlvi.

next century Robert Grant added to the corpus with "O worship the King."

6's and 4's mix well into fine dactylic verse. The best examples are in 664.6664., which is the skeleton of the following:

"Come, Thou almighty King"
"My country, 'tis of thee"
"My faith looks up to Thee"
"Shepherd of tender (eager) youth"

Tunes in triple time are the most satisfactory. A tune such as "Olivet" for "My faith looks up to Thee" becomes wearisome because it prevents the text from moving at a dactylic pace. "Bread of Life" (64.64.D.) suffers for the same reason, plus the fact that dactyls are inappropriate for the subject matter—understanding the Word of God. Likewise, "Nearer, my God, to Thee" has become a funeral dirge with "Bethany" (usually put into 6/4 time); yet Sarah Adams wisely chose dactylic movement to indicate the hope and aspiration which undergird the text. Try reading the following lines from the fifth stanza with a pronounced accent as marked, and notice the exuberance:

Ór if, on jóyful wing
Cléaving the skȳ,
Sún, moon, and stárs forgot,
Úpward I flý.

No funeral this!

That dactyls can be dangerous is shown in the third stanza of "No, not despairingly" by Horatius Bonar. If there is one thing the meter does not convey, it is confession.

Lord, I confess to Thee
  Sadly my sin;
All I am tell I Thee,
  All I have been:
Purge Thou my sin away,
Wash Thou my soul this day;
  Lord, make me clean.

Nothing can redeem this mismatch of meter and matter from failure. Another mistake is "Master, no offering Costly and sweet," which is difficult to list in a service bulletin because of its strange first line. And there are serious problems in singing Lucy Larcom's

Draw Thou my soul, O Christ,
  Closer to Thine;
Breathe into every wish
  Thy will divine!
Raise my low self above,
Won by Thy deathless love;
  Ever, O Christ, through mine
  Let Thy life shine

with its insistent dactyls to Sullivan's equally insistent and monotonous 4/4 tune, "St. Edmund." When both the meter and tune are wrong for the intent of the text, any result and response can only be weak and ineffective.

Both dactylic and anapaestic meters are based on triplet movement; therefore it is only natural that they are best used in long texts. Thus the numbers are either "odd" or "large." Although *The Methodist Hymnal* classifies "Come, let us anew" by Charles Wesley as Irregular meter, it is actually 5 5 5.11.D. See stanza two:

> Our life is a dream;
> Our time, as a stream,
> Glides swiftly away,
> And the fugitive moment refuses to stay.
> The arrow is flown,
> The moment is gone;
> The millennial year
> Ruhes on to our view, and eternity's here.

As a descriptive meter it is perfect for picturing the years rolling by in swift succession. It may be unsingable by a congregation, but it is a choice illustration of the use of the proper meter for the subject matter.

Another text, anapaestic, in 669.D., is Wesley's

> O how happy are they
> Who the Saviour obey,
> And have laid up their treasure above!
> Tongue can never express
> The sweet comfort and peace
> Of a soul in its earliest love.

Such hymns suggest that these meters should be called the Meters of Urgency or of Rapture. There is headlong dash, religious fervor, even ecstasy in such meters.

It would be hard to find a more ecstatic hymn passage than the following 11 8. 11 8. by Joseph Swain:

> O Thou, in whose presence my soul takes delight,
> On whom in affliction I call,
> My comfort by day, and my song in the night,
> My hope, my salvation, my all!
>
> He looks! and ten thousands of angels rejoice,
> And myriads wait for His word;
> He speaks! and eternity, filled with His voice,
> Re-echoes the praise of the Lord.

It is also possible to put the same kind of movement into a series of eight 8's, but hymns such as "How tedious and tasteless the hours" have become tedious and tasteless.

An interesting historical item of hymnody is John Bunyan's poem "He who would valiant be" in the dactylic 65.65. 666.5.

> He who would valiant be
> 'Gainst all disaster,
> Let him in constancy
> Follow the Master.
> There's no discouragement
> Shall make him once relent
> His first avowed intent
> To be a pilgrim.

The tune "Monk's Gate" is a misfit, since it has no triplet feeling, but rather is iambic in nature and depends on a tied over note at two cadences.

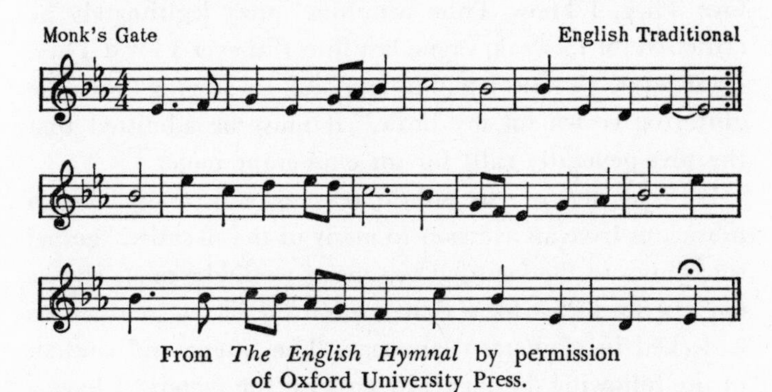

From *The English Hymnal* by permission of Oxford University Press.

Canon Winfred Douglas captured the exact spirit of meter and text in his tune "St. Dunstan's":

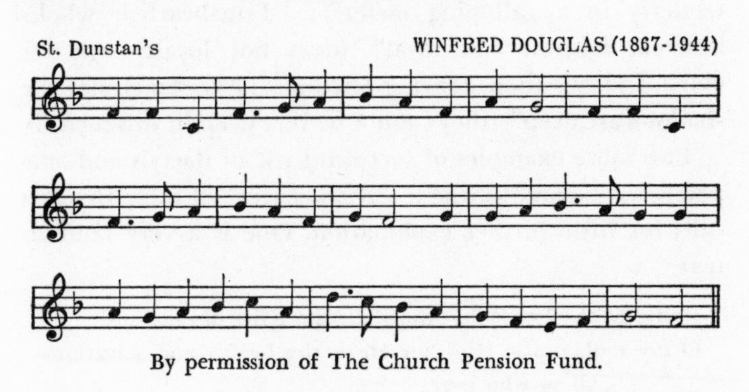

By permission of The Church Pension Fund.

Four 11's is a favorite dactylic meter, and two excellent and familiar examples are "Immortal, invisible, God only wise" and "How firm a foundation, ye saints of the Lord." The Christmas children's hymn "Away in a manger, no crib for a bed" is in the same meter. While "Lord Jesus, I love Thee, I know Thou art mine" may legitimately be criticized for its weak, vague last line ("If ever I lov'd Thee, Lord Jesus, 'tis now") and its emphasis on singing "with the glittering crown on my brow," it must be admitted that the text generally calls for an exuberant meter.

Perhaps one of the subtle reasons why many church musicians have an aversion to many of the so-called "gospel songs" lies in the fact that too many would-be poets choose dactylic forms for ideas that are frankly incongruous when bedecked in exuberant language. The intent and content of the following do not really go with the meter: "I have a Saviour, He's pleading in glory" (pleading in triplet movement?); "Softly and tenderly Jesus is calling" (softly and tenderly in a galloping meter?); "True-hearted, whole-hearted, faithful and loyal" (does not loyalty call for martial rather than dancing rhythm?); "O sometimes the shadows are deep" (they cannot be very deep in this meter!)

Two more examples of successful use of dactyls and anapaests will suffice, for the infectious nature of these rhythms calls for little further explanation. One is a very familiar text,

Praise to the Lord, the Almighty, the King of creation!
O my soul, praise Him, for He is thy health and salvation!
All ye who hear,
Now to His temple draw near;
Join me in glad adoration

with one of the longest opening lines in hymnody. The meter is 14.14. 4 7. 8. in dactyls, and is ideal for the burst of praise and adoration. The second is a fairly unfamiliar text,

> There's a voice in the wilderness crying,
> A call from the ways untrod:
> Prepare in the desert a highway,
> A highway for our God!
> The valleys shall be exalted,
> The lofty hills brought low;
> Make straight all the crooked places,
> Where the Lord our God may go

by James L. Milligan, with all the thrust of anapaestic movement. The singer is hurled from accent to accent as the urgent call of the prophet is heard. The meter is listed as Irregular since the anapaestic movement does not continue for long; instead, iambic movement gradually takes over. Thus the hymn serves as a bridge to the next category, that of mixed meters.

V. MIXED METERS

There are two basic kinds of mixed meters used in hymnody. We have just seen one, where anapaests turn into iambic. How does this happen? Fundamentally, an anapaest is an iamb with an added pulse for upbeat:

Iambic: ∪ /
Anapaestic: ∪ ∪ /

In the same way a dactyl is a trochee with an added falling pulse:

Trochaic: /∪
Dactylic: /∪∪

To end a hymn, a strong accent is desirable, so even dactylic hymns yield to anapaestic endings. Take the line, "Immortal, invisible, God only wise." Percy Dearmer, *Songs of Praise Discussed,* says, "The classical *dactyl* /∪∪ is more generally supplanted in English verse by the *anapaest* ∪∪/, but the foot is nearly always shortened in some part or parts of the line, e.g.,

∪ / | ∪ ∪ / | ∪∪ / | ∪∪ /
| Immor | tal, invis | ible, God | only wise." [1]

Therefore the editor lists this hymn as anapaestic; but it is just as reasonable to think of this as a mixed line—an iambic upbeat followed by a series of dactyls, ending on a strong pulse.

∪ | / ∪ ∪ | / ∪∪ | / ∪∪ | /
Im | mortal, in | visible, | God only | wise.

The only difference lies in placing the barline and accent to coincide with the musical accents. The same book lists "Be thou my vision, O Lord of my heart" as anapaestic, even though there are no two preliminary upbeats!

There is very little real difference in these two meters so long as the triplet movement remains constant, and it would

[1] (London: Oxford University Press, 1932), p. xxx.

be fruitless to argue which interpretation is correct. The point here is that both meters lend themselves to alterations at beginnings and cadences. A similar problem arises in an occasional iambic hymn such as

For the might of Thine arm we bless Thee,
Our God, our fathers' God;
Thou hast kept Thy pilgrim people
By the strength of Thy staff and rod;
Thou hast called us to the journey
Which faithless feet ne'er trod;
For the might of Thine arm we bless Thee:
Our God, our fathers' God.

The meter is listed as Irregular, and at first glance it would seem that anapaests are in evidence; but study of the second stanza reveals the hymn is basically iambic 76.76.D. with subdivision of several upbeats in the style of the English ballads:

For the love of Christ constraining,
That bound their hearts as one;
For the faith in truth and freedom
In which their work was done;
For the peace of God's evangel
Wherewith their feet were shod;
For the might of Thine arm we bless Thee:
Our God, our father's God.

Such mixing of meters is not so important a problem as it first appears; untrained singers have little difficulty in adding the extra syllables since they are usually unimportant and glide by quickly. A much more subtle form of mixing occurs in the delightful Polish carol, "Infant holy, Infant lowly." The music begins:

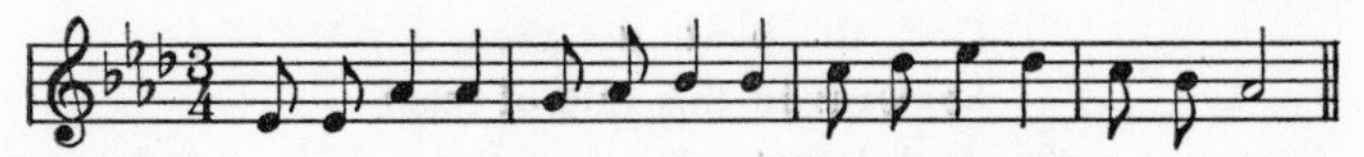

When the carol is sung or played, the organist says, "Ah! a mistake! The barline should be after the word 'Infant' with the accent falling on 'ho-.'" But look at the text again—it is not anapaestic; it is pure trochaic. Therefore the accent *does* fall on "In-." So we have a subtle anapaestic tune with a trochaic text, and the barlines are correct.

The second kind of mixed meter is more fundamental and involves the use of two different designs in one hymn. When both iambic and trochaic lines are found in a single hymn, the result is paradoxical; for the two meters are as positive is to negative. Yet in the hands of a skilful poet the change is made so easily that the singer is hardly aware. The metrical form 76.76.777.6. has been called the Wesleyan meter, for Charles used it for some of his finest and most striking poems. The 7's are trochaic, but yield to iambic 6's. The three trochaic 7's in the second half sustain the excitement and sustain drive at the very moment when dullness might begin. Note in the following example by Wesley how the words of lines two, four, and eight reflect the gentler movement of iambic to match the mood of the text:

Glory be to God on high,
(2) And peace on earth descend:
God comes down, He bows the sky,
(4) And shows Himself our Friend:
God th' invisible appears:
God, the blest, the great I AM,
Sojourns in this vale of tears,
(8) And Jesus is His name.

Robert Seagrave's

Rise, my soul, and stretch thy wings,
Thy better portion trace;
Rise from transitory things
Toward heaven, thy native place:
Sun, and moon, and stars decay;
Time shall soon this earth remove;
Rise, my soul, and haste away
To seats prepared above

in the same meter is occasionally found in hymnals, and the tune "Amsterdam" from the *Foundery Collection,* 1742, is a choice tune in this strange and fascinating mixed pattern.

"O Morning Star, how fair and bright," known as the Queen of Chorales, is the reverse pattern, starting iambic and ending trochaic. The meter is 887.887.4.8.4.8 with the interesting rhyme scheme of AABCCBDEEFF.

(Iambic) O Morning Star, how fair and bright
Thou beamest forth in truth and light!

O Sovereign meek and lowly!
Thou Root of Jesse, David's Son,
My Lord and Master, thou hast won
My heart to serve thee solely!
(Trochaic) Thou art holy,
Fair and glorious, all-victorious,
Rich in blessing,
Rule and might o'er all possessing.

The gentleness of the first six lines is neatly balanced by the strength and directness of the last four lines. In general, German chorales tend to be much more adventuresome in metrical designs than English hymns and hymn tunes.

Two familiar hymns combining dactylic and trochaic bring the discussion of mixed meters to a close. One is

Fairest Lord Jesus,
Ruler of all nature,
O Thou of God and man the Son,
Thee will I cherish,
Thee will I honor,
Thee, my soul's Glory, Joy, and Crown

in the unusual meter, 568.558.

The tune "St. Elizabeth" hides the dactyls to some extent by using ♩ ♩ ♩ and the total effect is of subtle warmth and joy ending in positive statements about Jesus. Mention has already been made about the Sapphic meter (11 11 11.5.) which is also a combination of dactylic and trochaic. (See p. 14.)

The second hymn is the campfire favorite, "God, that

madest earth and heaven" in 84.84.8884. The first line is purely trochaic, but the groups of dactylic fours give a pleasant relaxation to the whole: Darkness and light; Unseals our eyes; O God most wise; etc. The use of mixed meters by Reginald Heber reflects the nineteenth century concern for poetic excellence, an excellence which sometimes overshadowed the content of the hymns.

VI. MODULATIONS AND POETIC DEVICES

In his excellent *Representative Verse of Charles Wesley* Frank Baker uses the word "Modulations." He says:

Any musician knows that if he remains in the same key for too long monotony sets in. This he avoids by modulations, passages in a different, though related key, passages short or long, obvious or subtly concealed beneath the melody, varying both with the occasion and with the technical command and musical sensitivity of the composer. The same kind of thing is true in verse. "Modulations," as we may call them, are obviously more necessary in longer lines and longer poems, which otherwise would degenerate to a jog-trot.

Hymns are in a peculiar category, since they are made for singing to relatively simple tunes, to which each stanza must conform. Hymn-writers in general, therefore, tend to ignore (or to remain in ignorance of) the values of modulation. The slavery to the tune is one of the very important reasons for the widespread assumption that hymns cannot be poetry, an assumption based on the (sometimes unrealized) nature of poetry as a constantly varying compromise between the naturalness of common speech and the artificiality of strictly metrical speech; at the one extreme lies prose and the other the hurdy-gurdy. It is broadly true that hymns with no modulation are as unsatisfactory for reading as those with excessive or violent modulations are for singing. "Modulation in moderation" is the motto for the hymn-writer with a feeling for poetry.[1]

One of the devices of modulation is the choriambus, a foot made of a trochee followed by an iambus. Charles Wesley uses it in "Soldiers of Christ, arise"—the opening line of a SMD hymn. At first glance it would seem that Wesley has his accents misplaced, but he has purposefully used a "modulation" to give additional strength to the energy of Short Meter. Reginald Heber has done the same thing in

[1] *Op. cit.*, pp. xlvii, xlviii.

Bread of the world in mercy broken,
Wine of the soul in mercy shed,
By whom the words of life were spoken,
And in whose death our sins are dead;

Look on the heart by sorrow broken,
Look on the tears by sinners shed;
And be Thy feast to us the token
That by Thy grace our souls are fed.

So has Edwin Hatch in the following:

Breathe on me, Breath of God,
Fill me with life anew,
That I may love what Thou dost love,
And do what Thou wouldst do.

The directness of "Breathe" and "Fill" calls for trochees, yet the consecration and dedication of self presented in the last two lines uses iambics to pile the thought up to the last word. Such modulations call for sensitivity in choosing music settings which recognize the shift in pattern.

There is more subtlety and craftsmanship in great hymns than meets the eye (or the ear). Poetic devices are sinew and muscle which surround the skeletal meter, but if the rippling muscles and effects are obvious and distracting, the cleverness of the poet kills the spiritual intent of the hymn. To say this is not to disparage or discourage the use of poetic devices, for great hymnody could not exist without them. There are countless types of metaphors, rhetorical devices, figures of speech, and forms of repetition which are to be found in abundance in the hymnal. The following list is by no means exhaustive, even if it may seem exhausting. Many words may seem strange (they indicate the classical interest in poetry), but the ideas are sound and useful as the illustrations will show.

They are listed alphabetically rather than in closely graded categories:

1. Allegory—A story used to explain or teach an idea. "Awake, my soul, stretch every nerve" uses a foot race as an illustration of Christian living. There is a "cloud of witnesses," and God himself presents the crown of victory.

2. Alliteration—Repetition of the same first letter or sound in a group of words. "Some sheltering shade where sin and striving cease." "Take from our souls the strain and stress."

3. Anadiplosis—Using words or ideas which end one stanza as the start of the next. A poor example, because the device is overused to the point of annoyance, is

Not so in haste, my heart!
Have faith in God and wait;
Although He linger long,
He never comes too late.

He never cometh late;
He knoweth what is best;
Vex not thyself in vain;
Until He cometh, rest.

Until He cometh, rest,
Nor grudge the hours that roll;
The feet that wait for God
Are soonest at the goal.

Are soonest at the goal
That is not gained by speed;
Then hold thee still, my heart,
For I shall wait His lead.

Excellent examples are found in "O for a thousand tongues to sing" and "Ye servants of God, your Master proclaim" where the ideas are subtly used as a means of continuity from stanza to stanza: grace-My gracious Master; Name-"Jesus! the Name"; etc.

4. Anaphora—Repetition of a word at the start of successive lines. In both "Come, Thou long-expected Jesus" and "Hark! the herald angels sing," stanza three, Charles Wesley starts line after line with the word "Born" to hammer home the idea of the Incarnation.

5. Antanaclasis—Repetition with a slight difference in meaning, or a change in direction of thought. In the last stanza of "Jesus, united by Thy grace" Wesley has the following lines:

And ever toward each other move,
And ever move toward Thee.

Subtly the movement of man to man is turned to movement of man to God. ("Inasmuch as ye have done it to one of the least of these my brethren, ye have done it unto me.")

6. Antistrophe—Repetition of a phrase in reverse. The most obvious example is the "One in Three, and Three in One" type of formula used in many Trinitarian hymns.

7. Antithesis—Sharply contrasted ideas set in balance. Isaac Watts contrasts God's immortality and man's mortality in these two stanzas:

O God, our help in ages past,
Our help for years to come,
Our shelter from the stormy blast,
And our eternal home!

Time, like an ever-rolling stream,
Bears all its sons away;
They fly, forgotten, as a dream
Dies at the opening day.

8. Apostrophe—Addressing inanimate objects or persons (usually dead). "O perfect Love" and "O Love divine and golden," both wedding hymns, are examples.

9. Chiasmus—The crossing of lines or clauses, from the Greek "Chi" or "X." In "All praise to our redeeming Lord," stanza three, there is the following:

We all partake the joy of one;
The common peace we feel;
A peace to worldly minds unknown,
A joy unspeakable.

Joy and peace are crossed with peace and joy. Bernard L. Manning, in *Hymns of Wesley and Watts,*[2] points out another hymn containing several examples of chiasmus:

> Just, and Holy is Thy Name,
> I am all unrighteousness;
> False and full of sin I am,
> Thou art full of truth and grace.

To this Frank Baker adds, "The chiasmus is one of the natural outworkings both of the essential paradoxes of the Christian faith, and of the antithetical processes of Charles Wesley's literary art." [3]

10. Climax—Ideas and syntax arranged in ascending order of intensity. A short example is "Ours the cross, the grave, the skies," but the superb example is taken from the last two stanzas of "Thou hidden Source of calm repose." In one sentence, the Christian is taken in his journey from creature comfort, through all kinds of adversity, to heaven itself.

> Jesus, my All-in-All Thou art:
> My rest in toil, my ease in pain,
> The healing of my broken heart,
> In war my peace, in loss my gain,
> My smile beneath the tyrant's frown:
> In shame my glory and my crown,

[2] (Naperville, Ill.: Alec R. Allenson).
[3] *Op. cit.,* p. xxxvii.

In want my plentiful supply,
In weakness my almighty pow'r,
In bonds my perfect liberty,
My light in Satan's darkest hour,
In grief my joy unspeakable,
My life in death: my Heaven in Hell.

11. Echphonesis—The use of the exclamation point for emphasis. Examples: "Jesus! the Name high over all"; "Alas! and did my Saviour bleed."

12. Epanadiplosis—Beginning and ending a line with the same word. "Hide me, O my Saviour, hide."

13. Epimone—A refrain. Again Frank Baker has a pertinent comment: "Wesley's use of the refrain really demands an essay in itself. He employed it in strict moderation, knowing how easily a refrain can become forced or feeble, or the cloak for poverty of thought or craftsmanship." [4]

It is worthwhile to compare and contrast the use of refrains in the following:

"O come, O come, Emmanuel"

"Rejoice, the Lord is King"

"O Love divine, what hast Thou done?"

"True-hearted, whole-hearted"

"Thou my everlasting portion"

14. Epistrophe—Repetition of a word or words at the end of lines or phrases. Note the use of "for me":

[4] *Ibid.*, p. xxxii.

And can it be that I should gain
An interest in the Saviour's blood?
Died He *for me,* who caused His pain?
For me, who Him to death pursued?
Amazing love! How can it be
That Thou, my Lord, shouldst die *for me?*

15. Epizeuxis—Immediate repetition of a word or phrase in the same line—"I'll never, no, never forsake!"

16. Hyperbole—A figure employing exaggeration. "O for a thousand tongues."

17. Hypotyposis—A vivid description designed to bring a scene clearly before the eyes.

See, from His head, His hands, His feet,
Sorrow and love flow mingled down.

18. Mesodiplosis—Repeating a phrase in the middle of successive lines. See under No. 14 the use of the phrase, "can it be," in lines one and six. The first is a questioning attitude; the last is that of wonder.

19. Metaphor—A word or phrase ordinarily meaning one thing used of another to suggest a likeness between the two; comparison.

Joy is a fruit that will not grow
In nature's barren soil;
All we can boast, till Christ we know,
Is vanity and toil.

20. Metonymy—Substitution for one term another closely associated with it, as in stanza two of "When on my day of life the night is falling":

> Thou, who has made my home of life so pleasant,
> Leave not its tenant when its wall decay;
> O Love Divine, O Helper ever present,
> Be Thou my strength and stay.

21. Oxymoron—Combining for special purpose words which seem to be contradictory. Two examples from Wesley are "confident in self-despair" and "Victim divine." The Christmas hymn "Glory be to God on high" by Charles Wesley has two notable pairs of lines:

> God th' invisible appears:
> God, the blest, the great I AM.

> Being's source begins to be,
> And God Himself is born!

22. Paradox—A statement containing two opposite ideas. See George Matheson's

> Make me a captive, Lord,
> And then I shall be free;
> Force me to render up my sword,
> And I shall conqueror be.

And of course there is that amazing stanza from "O for a thousand tongues":

Hear Him, ye deaf; His praise, ye dumb,
  Your loosened tongues employ;
Ye blind, behold your Saviour come;
  And leap, ye lame, for joy.

23. Parenthesis (or a dash)—Explaining, qualifying, or completing information. See No. 14, lines two and three. Charles Wesley was fond of putting in parenthetical phrases as a means of expressing wonder or shock at the boldness of the gospel.

24. Personification—Abstractions treated as if they have human attributes. "Rise, my soul, and stretch thy wings," or stanza four of "Father of Jesus Christ, my Lord":

Faith, mighty faith, the promise sees,
  And looks to that alone;
Laughs at impossibilities,
  And cries, "It shall be done!"

25. Rhetorical question—The answer is obvious, and no answer is expected. See No. 14 again, which is one long rhetorical question: "And can it be that I should gain."

26. Simile—Unlike objects are compared in one aspect. See stanza two of "Rise, my soul, and stretch thy wings":

Rivers to the ocean run,
  Nor stay in all their course;
Fire ascending seeks the sun;
  Both speed them to their source:
So a soul that's born of God,

Longs to view His glorious face,
Forward tends to His abode,
To rest in His embrace

or

As pants the hart for cooling streams,
When heated in the chase,
So longs my soul, O God, for Thee,
And Thy refreshing grace.

27. Synecdoche—A part is used instead of the whole. "The mournful, broken hearts rejoice" or "O Sacred Head, now wounded."

28. Tautology—Repeating the same thing in other words. "His kingdom is glorious, and rules over all." See stanza two of "Jesus, united by thy grace":

Help us to help each other, Lord,
Each other's cross to bear;
Let each his friendly aid afford,
And feel his brother's care.

VII. CONCLUSION

Our excursion has taken us on an anatomical tour of hymnody. We have seen how the framework or skeleton of a hymn is dependent on the choice of the right meter and accent. We have seen how various poetic devices frame the sinews and muscles and determine shape and form. But we still have not plumbed the soul of hymnody. The spirit of hymnody is found in movement—in development of Christian concepts. Its purpose is not the creation of an aura or mood of vague "spiritual emotion" or that Sunday-nightish feeling which Erik Routley calls most dangerous; but rather development of thought along scriptural and theological lines, using those poetic devices which will speed the process and make vivid the imagery. Poetry thus is the handmaid of Piety and not a god to be adored or worshiped.

Frank Baker makes the pungent observation that Charles Wesley "wrote . . . because he *had* to, not mainly because he wanted to provide singable spiritual ditties for the people called Methodists." [1] Perhaps in this sentence lies the clue for today's mystery—why are great hymns not being written? We have no song we must sing, no faith strong enough to share, no hope that leaps over woe, no love which overflows to others. One does not sit down and say, "Today I think I shall write a hymn." Great hymns can be created only when poetic gifts and techniques are so developed that God's Spirit can flow through the mind, heart, and hand of a poet-Christian who must sing of God's grace.

Singing praise to God is a matter of no small importance. "Love so amazing, so divine, Demands my soul, my life, my all." Unless the hymns we sing become our personal expressions, and the thoughts expressed become our own thoughts, our worship will be vain before God. In I Cor. 14:15 Paul holds up the ideal toward which all must strive: "I will sing with the spirit, and I will sing with the understanding also."

[1] *Op. cit.*, p. liv.

INDEX

METRICAL INDEX

$2.75

THE ANATOMY OF HYMNODY

Austin C. Lovelace

Many hymnologists today are concerned with the quality of the hymns currently being written. They feel that most contemporary hymnists reveal a definite lack of understanding and appreciation of the poetic forms involved in hymnology.

With hope for a renewed understanding of the structure of hymnody, Dr. Lovelace provides for the first time a study of poetic forms as they are related to the expression of feeling and mood in hymn texts. Dealing simply with basic metrical patterns of hymnody, such as common meter, long meter, etc., he shows the best examples of each type and the reason behind the selection of this type as a vehicle for the thought of the text.

Instead of getting bogged down in the lives and influences of the classical hymn writers, THE ANATOMY OF HYMNODY presents a straight-to-the-point guide to hymns—their structure and meaning.